[It] INCANDESCENT

[It] INCANDESCENT

Amy Pence

Spence
4/2018

To Thomas
with gratitude ~
A.

ninebark

ISBN-13: 978-0-9791320-6-3
ISBN-10: 0-9791320-6-1

Cover Design: Lou Robinson
Book Design: Hailey Rabdau

ninebark

Rome, GA & Salt Lake City, UT
ninebarkpress.org

Ninebark Press is sponsored by the Rome Area Council for the
Arts. Tax-deductible contributions designated for Ninebark Press
may be addressed to Ninebark Press/RACA, 3 Central Plaza, Suite
359, Rome, GA 30161.

TO LINDSAY & MY SUE—

your statures touch the skies

The poems to follow are the works of a fictional speaker. Italicized lines are from the poems and letters of Emily Dickinson. The author has also taken liberties with the details of Dickinson's life derived from her reading of several texts, noted at the end of the book. Characters in the book, therefore, are either the products of the author's imagination or used in a fictitious manner. Enter [It] with the knowledge that the resemblance to actual persons is of coincidence only.

TABLE OF CONTENTS

Oh, did I offend it? [Didn't it want me to tell the Truth] Daisy —Daisy— offend it-
...who only asks – a task – [who] something to do for the love of It -

from The Master Letters

Called Back. It's what her headstone says. The Dark ocellated.
I recollect, orient. Summer in Amherst, near Emily Dickinson's
grave. Headstones teethe the new dusk.

She: my obsession. Her biography, the poems I write.
Knowing what she knew, what I once knew.

Here, I think, to research Emily. Or to find someone? Tread
the light gravel. Called back, it seems, looking for the path between.

BIOGRAPHICAL INDEX

Where to go in the pine -
fringed tunnel to nothing?

Nobody, No Man, No News, Nor
History—A Bodiless Campaign

That It reveals itself
as multiplicity—preemptory

locked down by trees in
loosened air - Not solitary—

Not teeming - sown
with a complexity - our

desires, the things It loathes—
the intimacies [It] will not share.

The life of Emily Dickinson, seductive to make our own. Her presence, her absence, may open a small box inside you. As a young woman, ED often trod the path. An archetype of thresholds, on her father's plot of land. From the Homestead, the path stretched to the Evergreens, home to her brother Austin and sister-in-law, Sue. Bowered by pine and cedar trees — a thread, a dash — *with just room enough for two*, ED wrote —

What portal do we enter? ED bids Sue goodbye as she leaves a party at the Evergreens. The houses are just one hundred yards apart. Moonless Amherst nights both black and still. Only stars drift. Perhaps Samuel Bowles, a frequent visitor to the Evergreens parties — usually without his wife — will witness her goodbye.

Is he the unknown Master? In photographs, Bowles burns his dark eyes, a dangerous full-bearded handsome.

Poetry as riddle - Obscurity
fondness for; sewing, see metaphor

Poetry and concision;
As consolation; aesthetics, terror

Face diffuse - bent to task
the seedbed, the bread, an urging

underground - Birds
obscure your mouth -

Here in Amherst, I skirt the periphery —

      pursued by all that came
      before I came to be —

      Arriving home to gaze at my face in the mirror — the
brittle blonde hair, the tired mouth — darkly spattered –

I considered the knife, found instead, the belt, the chair

I heard the Buckle snap -
My *Lifetime folding up,* and then the *letting go –*

So long ago - *and so of larger - Darknesses* - a then:

      At the periphery of trauma, can we ever conceal the
self? I am now fragmented — a fragment. Seek some
answer —

      Do I read each of her poems anew, knowing what I
knew? Did I come to find Emily or will I find my daughter's
story an involution of Emily's –

      And so, you find me: *a Nobody,* like Emily, living here
in the Dark, pushing my poems into your hands.

And what of *It?* Not he, not she, but the [It] to which ED kneels/knows: will grow small, grow large, will to [its] wondrous Be.

Found by her sister Lavinia or her maid Maggie, over a thousand hand-bound poems and drafts of letters addressed to an unknown "Master." Whether discovered in a drawer or a trunk, they were not burned as ED wished.

Penciled with alternative words, marked by all she omits, the drafts numbered just three. Possibly the final copies were sent, but to whom?

There, in the Master Letters (claims the biographer Sewall) lay the *matrix*, the *seedbed* for all the tropes and images of her poems.

Truth: 'slant,' 'must dazzle
gradually,' 'rare commodity';

When I state myself, as the Representative of the Verse
—it does not mean—me—but a supposed person—

to find what's missing – the 'potent
core' - poems remove

what skull I have—open
in moonlight—secrete ecstasy

opon+

+ = see my numerous, numinous
alterations —

see what I would have said, had
I said it as she did.

What we cannot find, slipping our voices into hers, Jay Leyda calls *The Omitted Center*. What ED declines to say "increases the privacy of her communication and our problems *piercing* that privacy."

Like others, like hundreds of
nobodies from everywhere/nowhere, I come
to the Dickinson house.

In the front parlor, following a tour
group, my bracelet breaks—indigo beads
scatter across Emily's wooden floor. People
turn, startled, look past me.

"What was that?" they say. One bead
lodges between the planks. I am absence—
a Plank in Reason, broke

Everyone wants to unstitch you:
from the Dark, don't I fathom you, pull your
unquiet face from the weave?

In your dash, Emily, I live between
skeletal, shot through –

Your mind turns on a wire - a spool
to undergird, adhere a lack

Shatter it to pieces as [you] do -
enflesh silence where I discover

sealed in *Prose* – [you]
put there to *keep Still* -

Of Dickinson's Dash: papers written, books —
whether a thread or a light to guide her through
the Dark —

                dialogic, polyphonic? Is it to
rupture / a gash to signal what's omitted?
Whether a suture to stitch [It], so much falls
between [within] the line —

                  an identity.

Now, unscrewed from flesh
in those breaking drawers of earth

- your facing effaced
– I Dash -

unwind the past,
unstitch the Dark in you -

A small figure passes, *wearing gay muslins in summer and bright merinos in winter* (she did not begin wearing white until 1861).

Fireflies. Slips of paper shift in her pockets.

Strange blooms arise on many stalks —
                    that heady summer of erotic
white

HOUSE UNEASED

First the bodice, then the strings —
then a tug at Circumference —

a mind with all its corridors,
its passageways: its own interior ghost

One need not be a Chamber — to be Haunted —
One need not be a House —

Here [we] stand in the Corporeal
in a room suffused with you —

ED at twenty-five. She's returned to the Dickinson Homestead, the house her family left when she was nine. Her father has finally regained his ancestral home, lost by his father, years before.

Squire Dickinson installed the copula on the roof, built the Evergreens for his son next door, encircled his acreage with hemlock trees, so that all might stay within (his circumference).

She sits at her writing desk. You can imagine the still, prim head with its tightly woven hair. You've seen that one picture: her quizzical mouth, eyes implacable.

Her hand moves across the desk, thinly constructed of cherry wood. Her figure obscures the window. Over her shoulder, the letter she writes:

I believe my "effects" were brought in a bandbox, and the "deathless me," on foot, not many moments after....Mother has been an invalid since we came home, and Vinnie and I "regulated," and Vinnie and I "got settled," and still we keep our father's house, and mother lies upon the lounge, or sits in her easy chair. I don't know what her sickness is, for I am a simple child, and frightened at myself....From your mad Emilie.

Under the house's eaves, the heart
beats in that *pause of space*, uneasy

You shift shining in a window—
  planks drop in the numberless afternoon

And then a Plank in Reason, broke,
And I dropped down, and down —

And hit a World, at every plunge,
And Finished knowing — then -

You: a dim house locked shut—
+ latching all your entries +

In the Amherst College Library, I am underground in the Archives and Special Collections. Here to see the facsimiles of her fascicles.

I peer over the shoulder of a researcher at the table near me. Unseen. The page stamped with the incorporeal letters of time that aren't yet mine.

Lean in to read the repetitions: *Dear Mr. Bowles, dear friend, Samuel Bowles, Bowles, to Bowles,* ED writes beseechingly. His eyes, I remember, bold.

Could race down your body, find the spot where the heat grows. To Mary (his wife, *that hysteric,* they say, *that toad*) ED wrote: *the heart wants what it wants —or else it does not care.*

Wasn't that what I did —my mistake —to forsake what others said about my X? Thinking I knew him – could know his mind? Compelled to his dangerous lie?

A page slips from the file, lands near the fragment of me, a Nobody in time.

[*Ourself behind ourself, concealed —*   ]

The self secreted in the self. Eighteen years ago, as our daughter formed inside me, he began to turn, my then-husband. Loathing my body filling with a her. My sadness was complete after Daisy was born: his tempers, his possessiveness. Not of me. Of her.

He said he knew he *should* love me. But he often grabbed her away, saying I was not good enough. Throbbed angrily, striking. Believed him, until I didn't. Fighting for air, after the divorce, I thought: if not husband, he was still her father. Daisy loved him.

Until her tantrums, her rages, beginning at four. The way she drew the figures armless: the bell-shaped mothers and girls.

The father with arms—
stretching through sky, finding their way into our house.

Don't make me go, don't make me go, Mama, she would cry. And more. She said more. That's when a part of me froze. Every time. *It's okay, it's okay*; I would soothe, I would say.

Out of love for her, he couldn't, wouldn't be cruel—
Or could he? —that unsaid, or the-could-not-say, at four.

EFFACED

Pages fall open, pages sewn —
a pinned waxwing, an exotica

Eyes – light claret in a glass —
Eyes unable to see — at last

I had no portrait, now, but am small,
like the wren; and my hair is bold,

like the chestnut burr; and my eyes,
like the sherry in the glass the guest leaves.

ED's small atoms sent to others: paper pinned with cut flowers, poems embedded in letters, slant words tucked next to her brown bread, her coconut cake, sent by basket to the back door of Sue's house by a servant. A collage of photos cut from local papers.

Letters framed the poems sent to Bowles, letters surreptitiously tucked within other envelopes, so her father wouldn't know. A play of words — redolent with the dash — a few letters trudged across the meadow under Mr. Sweetser's hat.

And what of the *speckled breast*?
Amputate my freckled Bosom!

What *blameless mystery* —
I have guessed –

A solemn thing — it was — I said —
A woman — white — to be —

Gaps now blackened – you penned
a mute traveler — unarmed —

On her father's embossed stationery, a caricature
takes shape. ED sketches her father leaving the
Capitol (a smokestack over a puffed-up man with
his "Whig" raised, his face masked).

She looks out her window, south towards the hat
factory —

       Holds [It] up, far from her face. During the
day, in bright light, her vision muffles, begins to fail.

He is armless, the man, retreating.

       She will send it to Sue.

The nobody writes all night
To scrawl [It]; the [It] effaced

- facing the effaced - his violence
screwed to the little wire [you] -

The errant page I slip into my notebook –[*a burglar! A thief!*] while the researcher regards her dry cuticles. When she turns back to her task: I watch her note the gaps, the blackened redactions made to Emily's letters.

Across the path from the Homestead—where I stood looking out the window – did I see that dark ghost self Sue? That one who would bathe Emily's body at her death, that one so estranged by the end that some say they had not spoken in years?

Didn't I run into that dusk on the path between the houses – through the cemetery –bathed on all sides by fireflies? I circled the houses, once, twice. Did I suppose Emily like my own daughter?

Yes. I read each poem anew, not knowing what I knew. If I am nobody, who are you?

Past her garden: crepuscular light. I almost see her bending there, the ghost Emily—the one gardening with an oil lamp by her side. She of the failing eyes.

Do we blind ourselves to what we do not want to see?

I shut my eyes —and groped as well
'Twas lighter — to be Blind.

To Whom Not any Face cohere
Unless concealed in Thee

Once taken in, nothing unmakes
your dry – uneven face

Years ago, in the past, a thing unspooled —
I denied, tried, said *no, he wouldn't do such a thing. Not to
her, not to whom he loves* -

only to run into full consciousness of what he
was doing, had done —

Though [It], undone, why the layers: his
voice — hearing him again — ?

A voice —Masterful, that I bent to - *who bends
her smaller life to his (it's) meeker (lower) every day* -

HER CUTLERY

Blades so slick they bend the fierce
to a follicle — words a Wilderness

She dealt her pretty words like Blades —
How glittering they shone —

And every One unbarred a Nerve
Or wantoned with a Bone -

a deeper primeval Dark – a *Belt*,
a *Bandage*, a *Goblin* folded

at the core — Yet, you cleaned
the cutlery — Yet, you baked

the bread - a daily *blank-to-*
blank, to please the lies

He put the belt around my life —
I heard the buckle snap —

And turned away, imperial
My Lifetime folding up -

Did Edward Dickinson see a version of himself in her? His granddaughter wrote later, innocently: "His daughter Emily reproduced him in more

than coloring of the hair of red bronze, the wine-brown eyes that could flash with indignation or soften in approval, that were common to both of them."

The Omitted Center.

Your mother —silent—
then paralyzed - what stuns

the stunning— but blades, Emily—
to bleed arrogance to bone + show

what hands a mother stows
when she's not been cauterized—

I always ran Home to Awe when a child, if anything befell me. He was an awful Mother, but I liked him better than none.

Didn't I, a Nobody, seek help: first the therapist who told me – Darkly - about fathers who groom their children, then said: tell her to say "no" to the Daddy, "No, Daddy, we don't do that." And so I said [It].
Told her to say *no*. *No, Daddy, no!* As if it was for her to say.

Silence + Shame + Omission.

To the police, she could only stare, say "no, Daddy. No."
Didn't I call the lawyer? Take him to court? By then there were only my words, not hers. What she said he'd done. What couldn't be taken back. Now omitted.

Her face was in a bed of hair,
Like flowers in a plot –
Her hand was whiter than the sperm
That feeds the sacred light.
Her tongue more tender than the tune
That totters in the leaves –
Who hears may be incredulous,
Who witnesses, believes.

Her body arched in the bath. An innocence: *Look what Daddy showed me*. What she would say he'd done, but only to me.

Zero at the bone.

Did I see what I saw?

Enforced visitations: *Don't make me go. Don't make me go!* My hand on her back to still her quaking. Then the smudge of her face through the car window, going.

My fault. Those words that shouldn't have been said? *Tell him: No, Daddy -*

From Blank to Blank —
A Threadless Way
I pushed Mechanic feet -

WHITE DRESS

Every gap – every closure
hook in eye - every mortifying sign –

Vesuvius let loose —red
lava, red-haired father.

Mother who lapsed - too missing to bear
your Terror. The dress, sutured

in the Dark - a signal. *What would
you do with me if I came "in white?"*

When ED stayed too late at Austin and Sue's parties next door, her father would stand at the far end of the path holding a lantern (*—just room enough for two*).

The morning after a party, ED cut out a picture of a figure being pursued by a "dragon-like creature with a forked tail" and scrawled a note to Sue:

> *P.S. Lest you misapprehend, the unfortunate insect upon the left is Myself, while the Reptile upon the right is my more immediate friends, and connections.*

— like the cutout you pasted flat
a reptilian father escorts you back

across the path. Your dress a white
burning whiter —your dash

keeps secrets soft: a breath, a pause,
A Secret told— Ceases to be a Secret

A slow walk in the Dark
what Secret *—that —can appall but One*?

Dickinson writes of her father's
absence after his death as
a *pause of Space*

    that I call 'Father'.

Housed in a glass cube at the top of the
Homestead stairs: Emily's dress. Other visitors move
about me, then vitrify—

Because I am delayed—seeing [It]—
the white dress.

Standing just beside, the planked back of a man
wearing an old-fashioned waistcoat.

Her dress—plain, buttoned at the front—large with
pockets – *a pause of space*—

Because her eyes gaze out the open pantry window –
caught– she wipes her floured hands on the white front,
lifts the paper – flattened back of envelope - from her
pocket, takes up the pencil nub to jot a line.

Because her father would eat only the brown bread
she made—

Because I judge she was no more than five foot
one—my height –

When the man turns from the dress, I startle from
his eyes. We see each other in death. His eyebrows
immense, wiry. I hurry from *Awe*.

EVERY CIRCUMFERENCE

One body in starlight—or two
snow in Amherst and sky

> Once, twice, Bowles, that dark dreamer, may
> have walked ED back home, the one to whom
> she wrote - late at night, looking out at snow
> gathering between two houses.

thinned to a crystalline skin—akin
to a [She] mottled by grief

One star falls falling—its tracery
lone as a broach at your throat

where you stand midway between
two houses—one the Evergreens—

hemlocks swollen
at the periphery of desire.

And later, summer, - those slow last
journeys alone. Leaves rush in wind
with fine atoms of death to seal them
in —

> *And so of larger – Darknesses –*
> *Those Evenings of the Brain –*
> *When not a Moon disclose a sign –*
> *Or Star - come out – within –*

The tour guide - I follow her every day - walks ahead along the path to the Evergreens, says "when Emily was alive, the hemlocks were only bosom-high" (she says it reverently, gasping).

What whispers do I hear as I traverse the path, straggling behind?

When a stone scrapes under my foot, the last, a college girl (looking so much like my daughter grown)

turns, says to her friends: *did you hear that?*

But no one hears. They go on.

See how the father stands
finite — holding a lamp.

You stood across in snow
vowed to enclose any opening.

What closes, opens - a hasp
the mind makes of the universe —

BOX OF PHANTOMS

A woman bends near her window,
working far into night - across paper

> Dickinson wrote to Sue: *If it is finished, tell me, and I will raise the lid to my box of Phantoms, and lay one more love in.* To her slightly older cousin, John Graves, she used the same phrase, sketched a tombstone.
>
> How the loves crowd in, then abandon her. Bowles would come later, when the box had been well-squared, built for a steady, prodigious burial.

her pen crosses, re-crosses —
her hair, its thatch — all

the follicles caught fast -
all the words unlatch into whorl

> Jay Leyda wrote of Samuel Bowles: "his joshing deflection of ED's emotion, especially as reflected in her poetry, may have altered her life."

The researcher — mouth pursed, thin —
approaches the archivist in the Amherst Special
Collections: *isn't there a memento mori: a curl from
Emily's hair?*

Come back tomorrow, he says. I leave with that
errant facsimile, the one the researcher missed.

Infiltrate me with your look -
across every battered century,

perched aloft in your cells —
the room — not a myth,

There is a pain —so utter —
it swallows / substance up —

but a longing for what is spare,
understood. – You,

collecting truth
in the grim box of self

So memory can step
Around – across – opon it –

What to do when I had to turn my daughter over
to her father every other week? Lie sleepless. When
home, she would curl on the sofa in a daze. Then slowly,
over the week, when I would least expect it, Daisy would
tell me more.

A system. A failure. But now there was nothing
I could do; she would tell no one else. *Nobody, No Man,*
No News, Nor History—A Bodiless Campaign. Is that when
I had to freeze parts of myself?

Where does One hide, when the child, too young
to lie, tells you what you feared and more?

How to stop the trance from coming on?
Collecting her horrors - a box inside -

Exhumed, your mind
like the boy shut out –

The Mouldering Playmate comes- ...
In just the jacket that he wore –

wandering gravely
Long buttoned in the Mold

Divided—by a world—
All that persists

dropped *—Bone by
Bone*, into that center-

unboxed

What playmate appeared to Emily? Standing close by the burying ground. To convince her that it is the living that are dead, and the dead that mourn us.

[IT] INCANDESCENT

Faces arrayed across
the battlefield at dawn —

They perished in the seamless Grass –
No eye could find the place –

Above them, the Good Death
hovers — that happen —

-        that   gap
before the slaughter —

Are we that wait —sufficient worth —
That such Enormous Pearl

As Life –dissolved be –for Us
In Battle's – horrid Bowl?

Imagine the swell of
the Master: grown immense

Daisy – offend it – who bends her smaller
life to his (it's) meeker (lower) every day

shifting small—red-slashed
wings on every blackbird—

More ignoble to die
with fear - than to make

bed, let it feed on you
like a tick— by degrees

It: that Memory you had to step around, opon. *It*, unnamed and unpersoned, made the *It* in Emily go to her knees –

At what cost our denial? How we go to our knees.

Like the box of phantoms, didn't I – the Nobody– have to box what was left of feeling – yet didn't [It] outgrow the box, when he did what he did, to de-construct my daughter?

Didn't He feed on who she was –

Didn't I say *no more*?

After ED's death, her sister Vinnie denied
the idea that their father was anything but
the grandest of men and while his occlusion of
their suitors was *wrong-headed, Emily's so-
called 'withdrawal from general 'society,'* for
which she never cared, was *only a happen.
Our mother had a period of invalidism, and one of
her daughters was constantly at home; Emily chose
this part.*

In the 19th century, and into our own, for
victims, Armstrong says, *incest was not the
taboo*…talking *about it…was the taboo* (qtd. in
Perriman 114).

The plume's body wavers, battlefields
render the fallen. Imagine the ruby -

Master — if you saw a bullet hit a Bird —
and he told you he wasn't shot- you

might weep at his courtesy, but you would
certainly doubt his word

stained white dress/   *the chest*
by and by *— to put the Alive - in*

ANOTHER MOLTING

The bones of the face —
As if knotted by thread

The bones white against dark
Night blooming Indian Pipes

like Cereus, cumulus cloud opon
which the patina of Her —

> Didn't Mabel Todd, mistress to Austin, paint the
> Indian Pipes, sometimes called the Ghost Plant, for Emily,
> and pass them under the door? Her breathing — halting on
> the other side?
>
> Didn't ED say nothing of [It]? Though Mabel
> made much of the Corpse Plant, chose the painting as
> cover for ED's book
>
> after her death. Didn't Mabel blacken the names,
> begin that century's task to obscure the whom and the
> why-
>
> her task – to take ED – her truth - apart?

A Supposed Person
stains the leaded glass

Like fascicles bound with thread: Would Emily come apart?

It is tomorrow. The archivist wears gloves, opens the black box: nested in one envelope, another.

She opens the folded origami sleeve -

The researcher peers in, her hair prickles to have me near. Our breath twinned, we watch the sterile fingers unearth Emily's curl. Bright: red-maple-leaf, a copper flash.

Startled by color, we sigh.

The archivist looks to me - I come apart.

I follow the dashes — all she had —*a filament, a law*— like that path through woods: a suture, a gap (for the secrets), slicked open with the thinnest blade.

Did I read each poem anew, knowing what I knew? Read them —felt each word under skin—

Memory rushes in —time-elapses —
I left with Daisy, went underground. Cut our hair. To make us small.

One by one— the poems leave
their bodies— was there enough

language for it? Air
hums through the bright

delicious bones - Double-jointed,
tousled from that century –

-   into the next – My stiff
and vicious pull at [It] -

Our cut brown hair - mine then hers -
clots the sink.

> But tis a single hair —
> A Battlement – of Straw -

What color? I asked. In the drugstore she
chose a box of copper-red, I, the blonde.

Found the safe house by internet, a
coalition for the abused, an underground
railroad. Discarded my job, my home –

        an identity.

In the car, her bright face in the rear view-
the freeway's enormous bowl, over the
state line

stopping at two different homes, two
different states, paying cash to rent –

someone's ransacked farmhouse

        Daisy runs into the bronze dusk
with her new hair, turning back to smile -

And then — the size of this 'small' life
The Sages — call it small —
Swelled — like Horizons — in my vest —
And I sneered — softly — small?

YOUR GNOME

That had the irreverent salutation —
that worded [It] rapt and singing

Could you, with honor, avoid death,
I entreat you, sir — It would bereave Your Gnome

that ruptured [It] thinning – What
light instigated all this bronze?

What was mown there – fair
by the Burying ground?

Posthumous, your voice not shorn
by the nor, late — or belated

I felt a Funeral, in my Brain
And Mourners to and fro

Here ED uses her posthumous
voice. Speaks to us from the dead,
even while alive.

I'm made vulnerable
to [It] —your lore —or perhaps

the spiked miseries of the self.
The *I* turns back

to the *supple suitor* —
Death, having issued its

stamen, its pistil —having unwound
the stiff knots of Who it was

your thought + omission
inspires -

Some say Emily suffered a
breakdown during the early years of the
Civil War —

1861-62: abandoned by those she trusted
her secret to —

Sue Dickinson (whom she called Dollie)
and Samuel Bowles (he called her Daisy)

Only Carlo, the Irish wolfhound, her
shaggy ally, loped beside her those years of
the *mad Emilie*

Why make it doubt – it hurts it so-
So sick – to guess –
So strong – to know –
so brave – upon it's little Bed
To tell the very last They said...
That Something – it did do – or dare
Offend the vision – and it flee –
And They no more remember me –
Nor ever turn to tell me why –
Oh, Master, This is Misery -

Amherst Cemetery: a sunset overbearing. Emily
entrenched and enclosed by an iron fence. Surrounded
by her Dickinsons.

A young man in a vintage uniform- perhaps not
to him -perches on a gravestone nearby. He gazes at a
girl placing a note and a small pebble on Emily's
headstone aside all the other notes and baubles.

When I turn, he vanishes, but the young woman
lingers: thick hair over one eye, looking past me, the
same college girl

—and yes, [it] is my daughter grown, years away
from when I saw her last. My sweat chills me —*because I
am afraid* -

Me: the Nobody that fled with her, my daughter,
and then was caught, arrested. The sheriff's car rolling
up the dirt road.

That Nobody would lose visitation *for a very long
time*, they said. I watched her, my daughter—seven by
then—through the Sheriff's car window leaving.
Eyes flat – unbreakable.

Fill me to capacity with fine ghost
roses—your gossamers filigree me

Ah, Necromancy Sweet!
Ah Wizard erudite!

Teach me the skill,
That I instill the pain

fulfill some futural past—
in the post-haste past-tense

how could we know
I have been in your Bosom

lodged like the dwarf rose
gnomic, crepuscular

Necromancy: the practice of communicating with the spirits of the dead in order to predict the future. What might Emily's dead have said?

In 1860, would the dead have foreseen how ED would love, would lodge herself—by word—twenty years later in the heart of Otis Lord, eighteen years older—the only man to return her passion, though he died four years into the affair

she following him close, in death—

The air crystallizes, like the grainy digits before sleep. I unfold that errant facsimile.

Out the window - interlocking trees, shorn of leaves.

Hadn't it been June when I first arrived? The note, written in the latter Emily—her letters fissured, like well-tied fishing lures: *Let me go for the day breaketh.*

No dashes, no knots, no stitches between the letters. I think of Bowles, to whom she would not write: *Let me go.* Whom she would never let go. The bowls of his eyes, empty after all.

Let her go—isn't that what I said at the last to Daisy's father, the X. On my knees.

Let her go—at last—

Since then —/ tis Centuries —
and yet Feels Shorter than the Day

lodged where [It] lies
where all the girls

go, tarnished - by time
where [it] licks the inside

of her legs - Skies burnish
I hear the same *noiseless*

noise -   an orchard
bearing down

Time nerves me – my ghost
opon the open way +

+Or did Emily write: "the way/
breaketh"?

When I look out the window again,
the path breaks open -

Mabel Todd of the Indian Pipes with
ED's editor Higginson would
"regularize" the poems after her death,
erase the dashes, ease what he had
named her *spasmodic gait* —

[it]s gaping truth

Vinnie and sister-in-law Sue (constantly
at war) obscured with different tales, to
keep [it] secret

Her family adapted, like most families
doomed to dwell there — the mother
sickened, the children to deny

To mummify, the insect winding
the carcass like so – Forgive me

I have no instruction, no alternative
life – just this one

The father's heart [*pure and terrible*]
abutted by woods, cautionary –

among hemlocked trees - Wither
the carapace that hid us -

My Splendors, are Menagerie —
But their Completeness Show
Will entertain the Centuries
When I, am long ago,
An Island in dishonored Grass —
Whom none but Daisies], know.

Beetles]

the shell crawling over with beetles –
the hand in – the hand out –

A Thrust – and then for Life a chance –
The Bliss to cauterize –

all the loaded nightdresses
hang ghastly on the line

Would he bend her to his will? Did I, a *Nobody*, like
the one to blind the Cyclops, see what could be done?

        She'd barely returned to the X –
        And, I, released

        waited until I knew she would be at her friend's,
waited in the Dark

The X took out his garbage, rolling the bin to the sidewalk
Behind him, many-fingered trees

        a streetlight,
when he bends briefly *"[stoops a] kneels a culprit"*

        I see the throat – throbbing –
             incandescent

        that gap, that held the lie
        that put the belt around her life –

If I am not your innoculant—
The Whole of it came not at once -

'Twas Murder by degrees -
then what am I? By dawn

I stare until you—milky-eyed
with death –   appear.

A Weight with Needles on the pounds —
To push, and pierce, besides —
That if the Flesh resist the Heft —
The puncture cooly tries —

[*I suppose the pride that stops the Breath, in the Core of Woods, is not of Ourself—*]

NOT OF OURSELF

Though the stoppage be difficult
be fragmentary, be torn — though

its bastard — ego — slips its ragged finger-
nail under the what-have-you -

I dash past your hard-earned caution
slant fellow, blistering

Winter in Amherst. Near the grave, time has played its wily games on me again.

My daughter, the college girl, one eye obscured by a dark lock, trudges by in snow. She places a note on Emily's grave.

She - so poised, so self-aware — a lake with depths no one but the I can see

The palimpsest that unfolds

surprised by new words rising

"Let me go for the way breaketh."

my interior ravaged - until
[It] listens - The rungs on

the fingers are the rungs on
the gate: some portal to

What if I say I shall not wait!
What if I burst the fleshy gate!

the conscious life —blued,
waits where I cannot see

[It], incandescent –

Her footsteps retreat across the ice. She, now grown —

wants me, finally, to go

that *blameless mystery* -

Did I save her? Did I mistake? Did I misconstrue?

No, Daddy, no.

No. [It] was her great love - like Emily's - to subdue

The pride, I see, was mine, was his, was of ourself

The path - now broken open -

When her father complained
about the nicked plate, Emily took it to
the garden to smash [it] open on a stone

Why?

So that he would not have to use [it] again

———————————————

After his death, she wrote, "his heart was
pure and terrible."

———————————————

My life had stood – a Loaded Gun –

THE POTENT CORE

That had at its heart the marksman—
that had at its breaking a war

That said It wasn't shot - though
it was simply a courtesy – a denial –

no more - That Daisy – that Dollie
– Deplored! Carlo roams

unmeadowed; That holds the hounds
barking, sees every secret to its core –

What shall I do —it whimpers so –
This little Hound within the Heart -

June again - dusk - fireflies just beginning. On the path I hear a ripping sound, a tear in the world

Will I walk through?

The dash upon entry

What is pure – terrible –

The Missing All - prevented Me
from missing minor Things.
If nothing larger than a World's
Departure from a Hinge –

From the back door, your bier borne
from the Homestead, enters the gaps

cut in fences – holds you aloft across
the grassy meadows *spreading wide*

Doom is the House without the Door —
'Tis entered from the Sun —

and then the Ladder's thrown away,
Because Escape — is done —

your *narrow hands to gather Paradise*
clutch a heliotrope – a knot

of field-blue violets and pink cypripedium
at your throat - coursing the path+

+Coursing the path, I go

      backward
      back along the path

      back through sun-stilled trees
            hemlocks coursing
            that mistook the *Nobody*, that ghost
                  that didn't know my course
                  the uncertain clot in throat

In this version, I
Release my ghost – the girl
      to the granular [it] of uncertainty
      frozen—the Indian Pipes—in dense wood

What was frozen in me
the *Nobody* knows how Daisy will go on –

traverse this life, know more than
we did - here in the Dark

[in her every atom

[engulfs us

Oh Sumptuous moment
Slower go
That I may gloat on thee —
'Twill never be the same to starve
Now I abundance see -

There, where the No –
daddy shone, the air grainy

like a skin –
Look -   an Amplitude –

ACKNOWLEDGMENTS

1110: "Biographical Index"

Drunken Boat: "Em Dash—"

Juked: "Effaced" and "Box of Phantoms"

New American Writing: "Another Molting" and "Daisies] Beetles"

Requited: "Your Gnome," "Not of Ourself," "The Potent Core," and "The Missing All"

IMPORTANT TEXTS

The work of many scholars has inspired and informed this book, including:

Crumbley, Paul. "Dickinson's Dialogic Voice." *The Emily Dickinson Handbook*, edited by Gudrun Grabher, et al., University of Massachusetts Press, 1998.

Denman, Kamilla. "Emily Dickinson's Volcanic Punctuation." *Emily Dickinson: A Collection of Critical Essays*, edited by Judith Farr, Prentice Hall, 1996.

Sewall, Richard B. *The Life of Emily Dickinson*. 1974. Harvard University Press, 1998.

Vendler, Helen. Dickinson: *Selected Poems and Commentaries*. Belknap/Harvard University Press, 2010.

---. *Poets Thinking: Pope, Whitman, Dickinson, Yeats*. Harvard University Press, 2004.

Italicized lines in the poems, used as epigraphs, and incorporated into biographical notes are excerpted from:

Dickinson, Emily. *The Poems of Emily Dickinson [Reading Edition]*. Edited by R.W. Franklin, Belknap/Harvard University Press, 1999.

Italicized lines may also be excerpted from:

Dickinson, Emily. *Letters of Emily Dickinson*. Edited by Mabel Loomis Todd. 1894. Dover Editions, 2003.

Individual lines appear from:

Leyda, Jay. *The Years and Hours of Emily Dickinson, Volume I*. Yale University Press, 1960, p. xxi.

Perriman, Wendy. *A Wounded Deer: The Effects of Incest on the Life and Poetry of Emily Dickinson*. Cambridge. Scholars Press, 2006, p. 114.

PERMISSIONS

Portions of The Master Letters were reprinted from THE LETTERS OF EMILY DICKINSON, edited by Thomas H. Johnson, Associate Editor, Theodora Ward, Cambridge, Mass.: The Belknap Press of Harvard University Press, Copyright © 1958 by the President and Fellows of Harvard College. Copyright © renewed 1986 by the President and Fellows of Harvard College. Copyright © 1914, 1924, 1932, 1942 by Martha Dickinson Bianchi. Copyright © 1952 by Alfred Leete Hampson. Copyright © 1960 by Mary L. Hampson.

Italicized lines from Emily Dickinson's poetry are reprinted from THE POEMS OF EMILY DICKINSON: READING EDITION, edited by Ralph W. Franklin, Cambridge, Mass.: The Belknap Press of Harvard University Press, Copyright © 1998, 1999 by the President and Fellows of Harvard College. Copyright © 1951, 1955 by the President and Fellows of Harvard College. Copyright © renewed 1979, 1983 by the President and Fellows of Harvard College. Copyright © 1914, 1918, 1919, 1924, 1929, 1930, 1932, 1935, 1937, 1942 by Martha Dickinson Bianchi. Copyright © 1952, 1957, 1958, 1963, 1965 by Mary L. Hampson.

WITH GRATITUDE

My thanks to several steadfast readers who gave me their feedback
and insight on drafts of this manuscript. My warmest thanks to Hajro
Terzich, Melissa Ginsburg, K.Dawn Goodwin, Julie Bloemeke, and
Valerie Martínez. The Hambidge Creative Residency program provided
me with the space and time to work on several versions of this book;
my appreciation for their wooded sanctuary for all artists. My heartfelt
thanks for fellow Hambidge Fellows Jerry Siegel for my author photo,
and Kevin Snipes for connecting me with the cover artist, Maggie Taylor.
As always, my thanks for the guidance of Sandra Meek, Michael Mejia,
and Mindy Wilson of Ninebark Press.

NINEBARK SUPPORTERS

Ninebark Press would like to thank the following people, and our many anonymous donors, for their generous support of this book:

Anonymous (multiple)

Christine Baczek

Allen Bell

Tina Bucher & Sherre Harrington

Jeanne Cahill

Curtis Clark

Katharine Coles

Thomas E. Dasher

Sarah Egerer, Brad Adams & Orgil
    Adams

Rupert Fike

Tonya Frehner

Alice Friman

Rick Glenn

Susan Goslee

John H. Graham

Susan Harvey

Jonathan Hershey

Mark Jarman

Kristine Jones

Karen Kao

Thomas D. Kennedy

Rod Kessler

John Lebowitz

Kathleen Lewis

Jeffrey Lidke

Michael Martone

Lesli Marchese

Michael McLane

Linda Meek

Mark Neely and Jill Christman

Josh Niesse

Lynn Pedersen

Scott Pence

David James Poissant

Katherine Powell

Jenny Sadre-Orafai

Natasha Saje

Andrea Sarvady

Larissa Szporluk

Alice Teeter

Lindsay Pence Todd

Sylvia Torti

Underground Books

Michael Walls

Jim Watkins

Federica Zanet Wilhelm

Rachel Schrauben Yeates

Thank you for supporting independent publishing and new voices in contemporary writing!

CPSIA information can be obtained
at www.ICGtesting.com
Printed in the USA
FSHW04n1530050418
46510FS